Basics of OAuth

Securely Connecting Your Applications

Preface

As technology continues to evolve, it becomes increasingly important to secure access to user data and resources. OAuth, an open standard for authorization, has emerged as a leading solution for secure authentication and authorization. With OAuth, users can grant access to their data and resources to third-party applications without sharing their credentials.

OAuth has become a widely adopted protocol, with major tech companies like Google, Facebook, and Twitter using it to secure their APIs. As such, it has become essential for developers to understand how to implement OAuth in their applications.

This book provides a comprehensive guide to OAuth, covering everything from the basics of the protocol to advanced concepts like token binding and multi-factor authentication. Whether you are a seasoned developer or new to the world of authentication and authorization, this book will equip you with the knowledge and skills you need to implement OAuth in your application.

The book is structured to guide you through the process of understanding OAuth, implementing it in your application, and avoiding common pitfalls. It begins with an introduction to OAuth, its history, and its key concepts, followed by a discussion of OAuth 2.0, the most widely used version of the protocol. The book also covers advanced topics like token introspection and token revocation, as well as emerging trends and technologies in OAuth.

By the end of this book, you will have a deep understanding of OAuth and how to implement it securely in your application. We hope this book will serve as a valuable resource for developers seeking to secure access to user data and resources in their applications.

A. Scholtens

Table of Contents

Chapter 1: Introduction on OAuth

OAuth (Open Authorization) is an open-standard authorization protocol used for granting third-party access to a user's data without sharing their credentials. It allows users to grant a third-party application limited access to their resources, such as their data on another website, without disclosing their login credentials. OAuth is widely used by web applications and social media platforms, such as Facebook, Google, and Twitter, to enable third-party authentication and authorization.

OAuth was first introduced in 2007 by Twitter, and it has since become an industry standard for secure authorization. It provides a simple and secure way for users to authorize third-party access to their data, without exposing their credentials or sensitive information. OAuth uses access tokens instead of passwords to grant access to resources, which are temporary credentials that allow third-party applications to access a user's data for a limited time. This approach significantly reduces the risk of account hacking and data breaches, as users do not need to share their login credentials with third-party applications.

The OAuth protocol consists of several components, including the authorization server, resource server, and client application. The authorization server is responsible for authenticating the user and issuing an access token to the client application. The resource server stores the user's data and provides access to authorized client applications. The client application is the third-party application that wants to access the user's data. The OAuth protocol uses a series of redirect flows and API calls to authenticate the user and grant access to the client application.

OAuth has several advantages over traditional authentication methods, including increased security, reduced risk of password leaks, and simplified user authentication. It allows users to grant third-party access to their data without exposing their login credentials, and it provides a standardized framework for authentication and authorization. Additionally, OAuth supports multi-factor authentication and role-based access control, which further enhance its security capabilities.

OAuth is important for several reasons. Firstly, it provides a standardized and secure way for users to grant third-party applications access to their data without sharing their login credentials. This means that users can access third-party services without having to create new usernames and passwords, which can be a cumbersome and time-consuming process.

Secondly, OAuth increases the security of user data by minimizing the exposure of login credentials. When users log in to third-party applications using their usernames and passwords, they are at risk of having their login credentials stolen or compromised. However, OAuth eliminates this risk by using temporary access tokens that are granted to third-party applications instead of sharing user login credentials.

Thirdly, OAuth simplifies the authentication process for both users and developers. By providing a standardized framework for authentication and authorization, developers can easily integrate third-party authentication into their applications without having to create custom solutions. This makes it easier for developers to create applications that work seamlessly with other services, improving the user experience.

Finally, OAuth provides users with greater control over their data. By allowing users to grant or revoke access to their data on a per-application basis, OAuth gives users more control over how their data is shared and accessed by third-party applications. This improves user privacy and helps prevent unauthorized access to sensitive data.

OAuth is an open-standard authorization protocol used for granting third-party access to a user's data without sharing their credentials. It provides a simple and secure way for users to authorize third-party access to their data, and it is widely used by web applications and social media platforms. OAuth has several advantages over traditional authentication methods, including increased security, reduced risk of password leaks, and simplified user authentication.

Its widespread adoption by web applications and social media platforms has made it an essential component of modern application development and user authentication.

Chapter 2: OAuth 1.0

OAuth 1.0 is the first version of the OAuth protocol, which was introduced in 2007. It is an open-standard authorization protocol used to grant third-party applications access to a user's resources without sharing their credentials. OAuth 1.0 uses a series of signatures and tokens to authenticate and authorize access, and it has been widely used by web applications and social media platforms.

Background and history of OAuth 1.0 OAuth 1.0 was first introduced by Twitter in 2007 as a solution to the problem of third-party applications requiring access to user data without exposing their login credentials. Before OAuth, users had to share their login credentials with third-party applications, which posed a security risk and made it difficult to manage access control. OAuth 1.0 addressed these issues by providing a standardized framework for authorization and access control.

The OAuth 1.0 protocol flow The OAuth 1.0 protocol flow consists of three main steps: request token, user authorization, and access token.

1. **Request token**

   The first step is for the client application to request a temporary token from the authorization server. This request includes the client credentials, the request token, and a signature that is used to authenticate the request.

   The first step of the OAuth 1.0 protocol flow is the request token. In this step, the client application requests a temporary token from the authorization server. This temporary token is known as a request token and is used to initiate the user authorization process. The request token is unique to the client application and is not tied to any specific user or resource.

To request a request token, the client application sends a request to the authorization server. This request includes the client credentials, which are used to identify and authenticate the client application, as well as the request token and a signature.

The signature is a cryptographic value that is generated using a combination of the client credentials, request token, and other request parameters. The signature is used to verify the authenticity and integrity of the request and prevent unauthorized access.

Once the authorization server receives the request, it verifies the signature and the client credentials. If the request is valid, the authorization server generates a new request token and secret key and returns them to the client application. The client application can then use the request token to initiate the user authorization process.

It's important to note that the request token is only temporary and can only be used to initiate the user authorization process. Once the user has authorized the client application, the request token is exchanged for an access token that is used to access the user's resources.

2. User authorization

Once the client application has obtained a request token from the authorization server, it needs to obtain the user's authorization to access their protected resources. This step involves the user being redirected to the authorization server to grant permission to the client application.

When the user is redirected to the authorization server, they are presented with a user interface that allows them to authenticate themselves and grant or deny the client application access to their resources. The user provides their credentials to the authorization server, which then verifies their identity and presents them with a prompt asking if they would like to grant the client application access to their resources.

If the user grants permission, the authorization server provides the client application with a verification code that confirms the user's authorization. This verification code is typically a one-time use code that is generated by the authorization server and is provided to the client application through the user's browser.

The client application then takes this verification code and combines it with the request token and the client credentials to request an access token from the authorization server. This access token is then used by the client application to access the user's protected resources.

It's important to note that the user authorization step ensures that the user has control over who is granted access to their resources. This helps prevent unauthorized access and ensures that users can trust the applications they use with their sensitive data.

3. **Access token**

The final step is for the client application to exchange the request token and verification code for an access token. This step is crucial as it allows the client application to access the user's protected resources.

To exchange the request token and verification code for an access token, the client application sends a request to the authorization server that includes the request token, verification code, and signature. The signature is a cryptographic value that is generated using a combination of the client credentials, request token, verification code, and other request parameters.

Once the authorization server receives the request, it verifies the signature and checks that the request token and verification code match those previously issued to the client application. If everything checks out, the authorization server generates a new access token and secret key and returns them to the client application.

The access token is a unique identifier that is used by the client application to access the user's protected resources. It is typically a long-lived token that can be used to access the user's resources for a specific period of time, after which it must be refreshed or re-authorized.

The access token serves as proof that the user has granted permission for the client application to access their resources. It is used by the client application to authenticate itself when making requests to the resource server on behalf of the user.

It's important to note that access tokens are typically more secure than request tokens because they are associated with a specific user and resource. This means that if an access token is compromised, it can only be used to access a specific user's resources and for a limited amount of time.

Signature methods OAuth 1.0 uses several signature methods to authenticate requests and prevent unauthorized access. The signature methods include:

1. **HMAC-SHA1**

   HMAC-SHA1 stands for Hash-based Message Authentication Code-Secure Hash Algorithm 1. It is a widely-used cryptographic algorithm that combines a shared secret key and the request data to generate a signature. The shared secret key is a secret value that is known only to the client application and the authorization server.

To generate the signature using HMAC-SHA1, the client application first constructs a base string that includes the HTTP method, the request URL, and the request parameters. It then applies the HMAC-SHA1 algorithm to the base string and the shared secret key to generate the signature. The signature is then included in the request as an authorization header or query parameter, depending on the OAuth 1.0 implementation.

The authorization server then uses the same HMAC-SHA1 algorithm and shared secret key to verify the signature. If the signature matches the expected value, the request is considered authentic and can be processed.

Example:

Imagine you are a developer working on a new social media app that allows users to log in using their Twitter accounts. To ensure the security of your app, you decide to use OAuth 1.0a protocol, which requires HMAC-SHA1 as the signature algorithm.

To get started, you first need to register your app with Twitter's developer platform and obtain the necessary credentials, including a consumer key and secret key. These keys will serve as the shared secret key that will be used to generate and verify the signature.

Now, when a user tries to log in using their Twitter account, your app sends a request to Twitter's authorization server that includes the user's authentication credentials and a signature generated using HMAC-SHA1 algorithm. The request includes a base string that includes the HTTP method, the request URL, and the request parameters, which are then combined with the shared secret key to generate the signature.

When Twitter's authorization server receives the request, it uses the same HMAC-SHA1 algorithm and shared secret key to verify the signature. If the signature matches the expected value, the request is considered authentic and the user is granted access to your app.

This process ensures that only authenticated users with valid credentials can access your app, and that the request data has not been tampered with during transit. It's a robust security measure that protects both your users and your app from unauthorized access and malicious attacks.

HMAC-SHA1 is a secure and widely-used signature method in OAuth 1.0, but it is not the only one.

2. **RSA-SHA1**

Another signature method supported by OAuth 1.0 is RSA-SHA1. Unlike HMAC-SHA1, which uses a shared secret key, RSA-SHA1 uses public-key cryptography to generate a signature that is used to authenticate the request.

RSA-SHA1 works by using a public-private key pair, where the authorization server has the private key and the client application has the public key. To generate the signature, the client application first constructs a base string that includes the HTTP method, the request URL, and the request parameters. It then uses its private key to apply the RSA-SHA1 algorithm to the base string to generate a signature. The signature is then included in the request as an authorization header or query parameter.

When the authorization server receives the request, it uses the client application's public key to verify the signature. If the signature matches the expected value, the request is considered authentic and can be processed.

RSA-SHA1 is a secure signature method that provides several advantages over HMAC-SHA1. One advantage is that the client application does not need to share a secret key with the authorization server, which can simplify key management. Additionally, RSA-SHA1 supports non-repudiation, meaning that the client application cannot deny making a request since only it possesses the private key.

Example:

Imagine you are a software developer working for a financial services company that allows customers to view their account balances and transaction history through a web application. The company wants to ensure the highest level of security for its customers' financial data, so you decide to use OAuth 1.0 protocol with RSA-SHA1 signature method.

To get started, you first need to obtain a public-private key pair. You generate the key pair using a tool that creates a public key that you will share with the authorization server and a private key that you will keep securely on the server.

When a customer tries to access their financial information through the web application, your app sends a request to the authorization server that includes the customer's authentication credentials and a signature generated using the RSA-SHA1 algorithm. To generate the signature, your app first constructs a base string that includes the HTTP method, the request URL, and the request parameters. It then applies the RSA-SHA1 algorithm to the base string using its private key to generate the signature. The signature is included in the request as an authorization header or query parameter.

When the authorization server receives the request, it uses the public key that you provided to verify the signature. If the signature matches the expected value, the request is considered authentic and the server processes the request to retrieve the customer's financial information.

One of the main advantages of RSA-SHA1 over HMAC-SHA1 is that the client application does not need to share a secret key with the authorization server, simplifying key management. Furthermore, RSA-SHA1 supports non-repudiation, meaning that the client application cannot deny making a request since only it possesses the private key. This ensures a high level of security for the customer's financial data and protects the company from fraudulent activities.

However, RSA-SHA1 also has some disadvantages. One is that it can be computationally expensive, especially when signing large requests or when the client application has many requests to sign. Another is that it requires a more complex key management system, since both the client application and the authorization server need to manage public and private keys.

3. PLAINTEXT

The PLAINTEXT signature method in OAuth 1.0 is the simplest of all the methods and does not provide any security measures. It is not recommended for use in production environments, and it is typically only used for testing purposes.

When using the PLAINTEXT method, the client application simply includes the shared secret key in the authorization header or query parameter without any encryption or hashing. The server then compares the received key with the one it has on record to authenticate the request.

Example:

let's say you are a software developer building a new social media app that allows users to authenticate and connect their accounts with other social media platforms using OAuth 1.0 protocol.

During the development phase, you decide to use the PLAINTEXT signature method for testing purposes to quickly and easily authenticate requests. To get started, you first need to generate a shared secret key between your app and the authorization server. This key is typically created during the OAuth 1.0 application registration process.

Once you have the shared secret key, your app can include it in the authorization header or query parameter without any encryption or hashing when making requests to the authorization server. The server then compares the received key with the one it has on record to authenticate the request.

The main disadvantage of the PLAINTEXT method is that it is vulnerable to eavesdropping attacks, where an attacker can intercept the request and obtain the shared secret key. This makes it unsuitable for use in production environments where security is a top priority.

4. HMAC-SHA256

Another signature method that is not included in the OAuth 1.0 specification, but is commonly used and supported by many OAuth 1.0 implementations, is HMAC-SHA256.

Similar to HMAC-SHA1, HMAC-SHA256 uses a shared secret key to generate a signature that is used to authenticate the request. However, instead of using the SHA1 hashing algorithm, HMAC-SHA256 uses the more secure SHA256 algorithm. This results in a longer and more complex signature that is harder to crack, making it a more secure signature method than HMAC-SHA1.

The HMAC-SHA256 signature method works by generating a signature based on the HTTP method, the request URL, and the request parameters, using a shared secret key. The signature is then included in the request as an authorization header or query parameter. When the authorization server receives the request, it uses the same shared secret key to generate a signature and compare it with the one received from the client application. If the two signatures match, the request is considered authentic and can be processed.

Example:

Let's say you are a software developer building a new online marketplace that allows users to authenticate and connect their accounts with other online services using OAuth 1.0 protocol.

You've been researching the different signature methods supported by OAuth 1.0 and have decided to use HMAC-SHA256 because of its added security compared to HMAC-SHA1. While HMAC-SHA256 is not included in the OAuth 1.0 specification, it is commonly used and supported by many OAuth 1.0 implementations.

To get started, you need to generate a shared secret key between your app and the authorization server. This key is typically created during the OAuth 1.0 application registration process. Once you have the shared secret key, your app can use it to generate a signature based on the HTTP method, the request URL, and the request parameters using the HMAC-SHA256 algorithm.

The signature is then included in the request as an authorization header or query parameter. When the authorization server receives the request, it uses the same shared secret key to generate a signature and compare it with the one received from the client application. If the two signatures match, the request is considered authentic and can be processed.

One advantage of HMAC-SHA256 over HMAC-SHA1 is its stronger security. Since the SHA256 algorithm produces a longer and more complex signature, it is more resistant to brute force attacks and other types of attacks. However, the longer signature can also result in slightly higher processing overhead and longer signature generation times.

Implementation examples

OAuth 1.0 has been implemented by many web applications and social media platforms. Some examples of OAuth 1.0 implementations include:

1. Twitter: Twitter was one of the first companies to implement OAuth 1.0. It used OAuth to allow third-party applications to access user data without requiring their login credentials.

2. Yahoo!: Yahoo! implemented OAuth 1.0 as part of its Yahoo! Social Directory API, which allowed developers to access Yahoo! user data.

3. Flickr: Flickr, a popular photo-sharing site, implemented OAuth 1.0 to allow third-party applications to access user photos without requiring their login credentials.

In summary, OAuth 1.0 is the first version of the OAuth protocol, which was introduced in 2007. It provides a standardized framework for authorization and access control and is widely used by web applications and social media platforms. The OAuth 1.0 protocol flow consists of three main steps: request token, user authorization, and access token. OAuth 1.0 uses several signature methods to authenticate requests, including HMAC-SHA1, RSA-SHA1, and PLAINTEXT. OAuth 1.0 has been implemented by many web applications and social media platforms, including Twitter, Yahoo!, and Flickr.

Chapter 3: OAuth 2.0

OAuth 2.0 is the successor to OAuth 1.0 and was designed to address the limitations and issues found in the earlier version. OAuth 2.0 is a more flexible and simplified protocol for authorization, with a focus on providing better support for modern web and mobile applications.

3.1 Overview of OAuth 2.0

OAuth 2.0 defines a framework for authorization that enables a third-party application to access a user's resources on a resource server without requiring the user to share their credentials with the third-party application. Instead, OAuth 2.0 uses tokens to grant access to the user's resources.

3.2 The OAuth 2.0 protocol flow

The OAuth 2.0 protocol flow involves four main actors: the client application, the authorization server, the resource owner (the user), and the resource server.

After the client application initiates the OAuth 2.0 flow by requesting authorization from the user, the protocol flow proceeds as follows:

1. **Authorization Request**

   The client application sends a request to the authorization server to initiate the OAuth flow. The request includes information such as the client ID, redirect URI, and the scope of the requested access. The scope indicates what types of resources the client application is requesting access to on behalf of the user.

2. **User Authentication and Consent**

The authorization server authenticates the user and requests their consent to grant access to the requested resources. If the user grants consent, the authorization server generates an authorization code and sends it to the client application via the redirect URI.

3. **Authorization Code Exchange**

The client application receives the authorization code and sends a request to the authorization server to exchange the authorization code for an access token. This request includes the client ID, client secret, and the authorization code.

4. **Access Token Request**

The authorization server validates the authorization code and issues an access token to the client application. This access token can be used by the client application to access the requested resources on behalf of the user.

5. **Resource Server Access**

The client application uses the access token to request access to the user's resources on the resource server. The resource server validates the access token and grants access to the requested resources if the token is valid.

6. **Access Token Refresh**

   If the access token has expired or becomes invalid, the client application can request a new access token by using a refresh token that was issued by the authorization server during the initial token request.

3.3 Authorization grant types

OAuth 2.0 defines several grant types, which are used to obtain an access token from the authorization server. The most common grant types are:

1. **Authorization Code**

   This grant type is used by web applications that run on a server. The client application sends an authorization request to the authorization server, which prompts the user to grant access. If the user consents, the authorization server issues an authorization code to the client application. The client application can then exchange the authorization code for an access token.

   Example:

   Let's say you're using a web application that needs access to your Google Drive files. When you first try to access the app, you're redirected to Google's authorization server to grant permission to the app to access your Google Drive files.

1. The web application sends an authorization request to Google's authorization server with the necessary parameters, including the client ID and the redirect URI.

2. Google's authorization server prompts you to log in to your Google account (if you're not already logged in) and then asks you to grant permission to the web application to access your Google Drive files.

3. If you consent, Google's authorization server issues an authorization code to the web application's server. This authorization code is a temporary code that can only be used once and has a short expiration time.

4. The web application's server then sends a request to exchange the authorization code for an access token, along with the client ID, client secret, and redirect URI.

5. Google's authorization server verifies the authorization code and issues an access token to the web application's server.

6. The web application's server can then use this access token to make authorized requests to the Google Drive API on behalf of the user.

This flow ensures that the web application never has direct access to the user's credentials and that the user has complete control over which applications can access their data. It also ensures that the access token is only valid for a limited time and can be revoked by the user at any time.

2. Implicit

This grant type is used by browser-based applications that run on a client device. The client application sends an authorization request to the authorization server, which prompts the user to grant access. If the user consents, the authorization server issues an access token directly to the client application.

Example:

Let's imagine that you're building a mobile app that allows users to access their social media accounts from a single platform. To do this, you need to integrate with the APIs of each social media platform (Facebook, Twitter, Instagram, etc.) and obtain access tokens that will allow your app to read and write data on behalf of the user.

To obtain these access tokens, your app will use the Implicit grant type. Here's how it would work:

1. Your app sends an authorization request to the authorization server (in this case, the social media platform). This request includes details about the

permissions that your app requires (e.g. read access to the user's timeline, write access to the user's profile).

2. The authorization server prompts the user to grant access to your app. This typically involves a web page or a pop-up window that explains what your app is asking for and asks the user to confirm.

3. If the user consents, the authorization server issues an access token directly to your app. This token allows your app to access the user's data on the social media platform.

4. Your app can now use the access token to make API requests to the social media platform on behalf of the user. For example, you might use the access token to retrieve the user's tweets or post a new status update.

The key benefit of the Implicit grant type is that it simplifies the authentication flow for browser-based applications like mobile apps. Because the access token is issued directly to the client application, there's no need for the app to store a client secret or perform the more complex server-side authentication flow used by other grant types like Authorization Code. This makes it a good fit for lightweight applications that need to integrate with third-party APIs.

3. **Resource Owner Password Credentials**

This grant type allows a client application to exchange the user's username and password for an access token. This is typically used in situations where the user trusts the client application with their credentials, such as in a mobile application.

Example:

Let's say you're developing a mobile app for a fitness company called FitTrack. FitTrack allows users to track their workouts, set fitness goals, and get personalized recommendations based on their activity level and health data. To access this information, users need to sign in to the app with their FitTrack account credentials.

To enable users to sign in to the mobile app, you decide to use the Resource Owner Password Credentials grant type. Here's how it works:

1. The user opens the FitTrack mobile app and is presented with a login screen.

2. The user enters their FitTrack username and password into the login form and submits it.

3. The mobile app sends the user's username and password to the FitTrack API server, along with a request for an access token.

4. The FitTrack API server authenticates the user's credentials and verifies that the client application (i.e., the mobile app) is authorized to request access tokens.

5. If the credentials are valid and the client application is authorized, the FitTrack API server issues an access token to the mobile app.

6. The mobile app uses the access token to make requests to the FitTrack API server, such as fetching the user's workout data or setting fitness goals.

In this scenario, the Resource Owner Password Credentials grant type is a good fit because the user is entering their credentials directly into the mobile app and is trusting the app with their FitTrack account information. By using this grant type, the mobile app can obtain an access token without requiring the user to go through a separate authentication process, such as logging in to a web-based authentication portal. This improves the user experience and makes it easier for users to access their fitness data on-the-go.

4. Client Credentials

This grant type is used by client applications that access resources that are owned by the client application itself, rather than a user's resources. The client application sends a request to the authorization server, including its client ID and secret, and the authorization server issues an access token directly to the client application.

Example:

Suppose you are building a web application that pulls data from a third-party API to provide users with real-time weather updates. Your application needs to access the API's data to provide weather updates, but you don't need to access any user data. In this case, you would use the client credentials grant type to obtain an access token for your application to access the third-party API's resources.

Here's how it works:

1. Your web application sends a request to the authorization server, including its client ID and client secret.

2. The authorization server verifies the client ID and secret and issues an access token directly to the web application.

3. Your web application uses the access token to make requests to the third-party API, such as fetching weather data for a specific location.

4. The third-party API server verifies the access token and responds with the requested data.

In this scenario, the client credentials grant type is used because your application is accessing resources that are owned by the application itself (i.e., the third-party API's weather data), rather than user-owned resources. The client application does not need to authenticate a user or obtain their permission to access the data. By using this grant type, your web application can obtain an access token directly from the authorization server and use it to access the third-party API's resources without requiring the user to authenticate. This simplifies the authentication process and makes it easier to access the data needed to provide real-time weather updates to your users.

5. Refresh Token

This grant type allows a client application to request a new access token by using a refresh token that was issued during the initial token request. This can be used to obtain a new access token without requiring the user to re-authenticate.

Example:

Suppose you are building a social media management platform that allows users to schedule posts, track engagement metrics, and manage multiple social media accounts in one place. To access the social media APIs that provide these features, your platform needs to authenticate with each API and obtain an access token.

However, access tokens typically expire after a short period of time, so you need a way to obtain new access tokens without requiring the user to re-authenticate every time the token expires. In this case, you would use the Refresh Token grant type.

Here's how it works:

1. The user logs in to your social media management platform and authorizes it to access their social media accounts.

2. Your platform sends a request to the social media API server, including the user's credentials and a request for an access token and a refresh token.

3. The social media API server authenticates the user's credentials and issues an access token and a refresh token to your platform.

4. Your platform stores the access token and refresh token securely.

5. When the access token expires, your platform sends a request to the social media API server, including the refresh token and a request for a new access token.

6. The social media API server verifies the refresh token and issues a new access token to your platform.

7. Your platform uses the new access token to continue making requests to the social media API server.

In this scenario, the Refresh Token grant type is used to obtain a new access token without requiring the user to re-authenticate. By storing the refresh token securely, your platform can obtain new access tokens automatically when the old ones expire, providing a seamless user experience and ensuring that the platform always has access to the social media APIs it needs to function properly.

Each grant type is designed to meet specific use cases and security requirements. It is important for client applications to choose the appropriate grant type based on their specific needs and the security requirements of their application. Additionally, OAuth 2.0 allows for custom grant types to be defined, which can be used to meet more specialized requirements.

3.4 Scopes

OAuth 2.0 defines scopes as a means to specify the level of access that a client application requires to the user's resources on the resource server. Scopes are strings that are defined by the resource server and can include permissions such as read, write, and delete.

Scopes allow users to grant different levels of access to different client applications. For example, a user might grant a social media application access to their profile information with the "profile" scope, but only grant a music streaming application access to their listening history with the "listening_history" scope.

When a client application requests access to a user's resources, it specifies the scope of access it requires. The authorization server then prompts the user to grant or deny access based on the requested scope. If the user grants access, the authorization server issues an access token that includes the requested scope.

Resource servers use scopes to enforce access control policies. When a client application makes a request to the resource server, the resource server checks the access token to ensure that it includes the appropriate scope for the requested resource. If the access token does not include the required scope, the resource server returns an error message.

In addition to the standard scopes defined by OAuth 2.0, resource servers can define custom scopes that are specific to their API. This allows resource servers to provide fine-grained control over access to their resources and enables client applications to request access to specific subsets of data.

Example:

Suppose you are building a fitness tracking application that allows users to track their workouts, set goals, and share their progress with friends. Your application needs to access the user's fitness data, but you don't need access to their personal information such as their email address or social media accounts. In this case, you would use scopes to request access only to the user's fitness data.

Here's how it works:

1. Your fitness tracking application sends a request to the authorization server, including the scope of access it requires. For example, your application might request access to the user's workout data with the "workout_data" scope.

2. The authorization server prompts the user to grant or deny access based on the requested scope. If the user grants access, the authorization server issues an access token that includes the requested scope.

3. Your fitness tracking application uses the access token to make requests to the resource server, such as fetching the user's workout data for a specific date range.

4. The resource server checks the access token to ensure that it includes the appropriate scope for the requested resource. If the access token includes the "workout_data" scope, the resource server returns the requested data. If the access token does not include the "workout_data" scope, the resource server returns an error message.

In this scenario, scopes are used to limit the access that your fitness tracking application has to the user's resources. By requesting only the "workout_data" scope, your application can access only the user's workout data and not their personal information. This ensures that the user's privacy is protected and that your application only has access to the data it needs to provide its features.

3.5 Tokens

OAuth 2.0 uses tokens to grant access to the user's resources. There are two types of tokens used in OAuth 2.0: access tokens and refresh tokens.

3.5.1 Access tokens

Access tokens are a fundamental component of the OAuth 2.0 protocol. They are issued by the authorization server to the client application and are used by the client application to access the user's protected resources. Access tokens are short-lived tokens that are typically valid for a limited period of time, ranging from a few minutes to several hours, depending on the configuration of the authorization server.

OAuth 2.0 defines two types of access tokens: bearer tokens and MAC tokens. Bearer tokens are the most commonly used type of access token in OAuth 2.0. They are essentially a string of characters that the client application includes in the Authorization header of its requests to the resource server. The bearer token serves as a proof of the client's authorization to access the user's resources.

3.5.2 Bearer Tokens

Suppose a user wants to use a third-party application to access their Google Drive account. The user logs into the third-party application and grants permission for the application to access their Google Drive. The third-party application then sends a request to Google's authorization server for an access token. The authorization server responds with an access token that is a long string of characters that represents the user's authorization. The third-party application then sends the access token with each subsequent request to access the user's Google Drive. Google's resource server checks the validity of the access token and grants access if it is valid.

Example of a bearer token:

> eyJhbGciOiJIUzI1NiIsInR5cCI6IkpXVCJ9.eyJzdWIiOiIxMjM0NTY3
> ODkwIiwibmFtZSI6IkpvaG4gRG9lIiwiaWF0IjoxNTE2MjM5MDIyfQ.
> SflKxwRJSMeKKF2QT4fwpMeJf36POk6yJV_adQssw5c

Bearer tokens are generally considered less secure than MAC tokens, as they can be intercepted and used by an attacker if they are transmitted over an insecure channel. To mitigate this risk, OAuth 2.0 recommends the use of secure communication channels, such as HTTPS, to transmit bearer tokens.

3.5.3 MAC tokes

Suppose a user wants to use a third-party application to access their online banking account. The user logs into the third-party application and grants permission for the application to access their bank account. The third-party application then sends a request to the bank's authorization server for an access token. The authorization server responds with an access token that is a message authentication code (MAC) that represents the user's authorization. The third-party application then sends the MAC token with each subsequent request to access the user's bank account. The bank's resource server checks the validity of the MAC token and grants access if it is valid.

Example of a MAC token:

    MAC id="h480djs93hd8",

    nonce="264095:dj83hs9s",

    mac="SLDJd4mg43cjQfElUs3Qub4L6xE="

In this example, the MAC token consists of an identifier (**"id"**), a nonce that provides replay protection (**"nonce"**), and a message authentication code (**"mac"**) that is calculated using a secret key shared between the client and the server.

MAC tokens are more secure than bearer tokens, as they use a message authentication code (MAC) to verify the authenticity of the token. As we see; MAC tokens include a timestamp and a unique nonce, which prevents replay attacks. MAC tokens are typically used in situations where the communication channel between the client application and the resource server is not secure, such as in mobile or IoT applications.

In addition to being short-lived, access tokens are also revocable. This means that the authorization server can revoke an access token before it expires, for example, if the user revokes their consent or if the client application violates the terms of service. Once an access token has been revoked, it can no longer be used to access the user's resources.

3.5.2 Refresh tokens

In OAuth 2.0, refresh tokens are used by client applications to obtain new access tokens after the original access token has expired. This allows the client application to continue accessing the user's resources without requiring the user to grant access again.

Refresh tokens are typically issued along with the access token, but they have a longer lifespan. The authorization server may choose to revoke the refresh token at any time, such as if the user revokes access to the client application or if the refresh token has been compromised.

When the client application needs to obtain a new access token, it sends a request to the authorization server with the refresh token included in the request. The authorization server verifies the refresh token and issues a new access token, which can then be used by the client application to access the user's resources.

It is important to note that not all grant types in OAuth 2.0 support refresh tokens. The Authorization Code grant type, for example, can be configured to issue refresh tokens along with access tokens, but other grant types, such as the Implicit grant type, do not support refresh tokens.

Refresh tokens can provide a more seamless user experience by allowing client applications to continue accessing the user's resources without requiring the user to constantly reauthorize the application. However, it is important for developers to carefully manage refresh tokens to prevent unauthorized access to the user's resources.

Example:

Suppose a user has authenticated with a third-party application and granted it access to their Google Drive account. The third-party application received an access token and a refresh token during the initial authorization process. The access token is valid for a limited time, typically an hour or so. After that time period, the access token expires and can no longer be used to access the user's Google Drive account.

However, instead of requiring the user to re-authenticate every hour, the third-party application can use the refresh token to request a new access token without requiring the user to enter their credentials again. The refresh token is typically long-lived, and can be used to obtain a new access token multiple times until it is revoked or expires.

Example of using a refresh token:

1. The third-party application sends a request to Google's authorization server to obtain a new access token, providing the refresh token in the request.

2. Google's authorization server verifies that the refresh token is valid and has not expired.

3. If the refresh token is valid, the authorization server issues a new access token and sends it back to the third-party application. The authorization server may also issue a new refresh token at this time.

4. The third-party application uses the new access token to access the user's Google Drive account.

Here's an example of what a request for a new access token using a refresh token might look like:

POST /oauth2/v4/token HTTP/1.1

Host: www.googleapis.com

Content-Type: application/x-www-form-urlencoded

client_id=<client_id>&

client_secret=<client_secret>&

refresh_token=<refresh_token>&

grant_type=refresh_token

In this example, the request includes the client ID and secret, the refresh token, and the grant type set to "refresh_token". The authorization server then responds with a new access token and optionally a new refresh token:

```
{

    "access_token": "<access_token>",

    "expires_in": 3600,

    "token_type": "Bearer",

    "refresh_token": "<new_refresh_token>"

}
```

The third-party application can then use the new access token to access the user's Google Drive account.

3.6 Implementation examples

OAuth 2.0 is a widely adopted authorization protocol used by many popular web and mobile applications to allow users to grant access to their resources to third-party applications. One of the main reasons for the widespread adoption of OAuth 2.0 is its simplicity and flexibility, which makes it easy to implement and use for developers and users alike.

One of the most popular implementations of OAuth 2.0 is Google OAuth 2.0. Google OAuth 2.0 allows developers to access Google user data, such as Gmail, Google Drive, and Google Calendar, without having to store the user's credentials. Instead, the user is prompted to grant access to their Google account, and Google provides the developer with an access token that can be used to access the user's resources.

Another popular OAuth 2.0 implementation is Facebook OAuth 2.0. Facebook OAuth 2.0 is used by many mobile and web applications to access Facebook user data, such as user profile information and photos. Facebook OAuth 2.0 allows developers to request specific permissions from the user, such as access to their friends list, and provides the developer with an access token that can be used to access the user's resources.

Twitter OAuth 2.0 is another popular implementation of OAuth 2.0. Twitter OAuth 2.0 allows developers to access Twitter user data, such as tweets, followers, and user profile information. Twitter OAuth 2.0 allows developers to request specific permissions from the user, such as read and write access to their tweets, and provides the developer with an access token that can be used to access the user's resources.

This approach is beneficial for both users and developers. Users don't need to create new credentials for every application they use, and they have greater control over which applications can access their data. Developers don't need to worry about managing user passwords or authentication, as they can rely on the authentication provided by the OAuth provider.

Chapter 4: Security Considerations

OAuth is an open standard for authorization that enables secure third-party access to a user's resources. However, as with any technology, OAuth implementations are susceptible to various security threats. Therefore, it is crucial to understand the potential security risks and take necessary measures to protect against them.

4.1 Threats to OAuth Implementations

1. Access Token Leakage

Access tokens are used to grant access to protected resources, and they are issued by the OAuth provider after a user has authorized a third-party application. Access tokens should be kept confidential and not shared with unauthorized parties. If an access token is leaked, it can be used by an attacker to gain unauthorized access to a user's resources.

Access token leakage can occur due to several reasons. For instance, access tokens might be transmitted over insecure channels or stored in plain text format on client devices or servers. Attackers can intercept these tokens, steal them, and use them to impersonate the user or perform unauthorized actions on the user's behalf.

To mitigate the risk of access token leakage, OAuth implementers should ensure that access tokens are transmitted securely and stored securely. Access tokens should be transmitted over HTTPS channels to prevent eavesdropping and tampering. Access tokens should also be encrypted and stored in secure storage mechanisms such as encrypted databases or secure key stores. Additionally, access tokens should be issued with an expiration time, and OAuth providers should implement token revocation mechanisms to revoke tokens that have been compromised or are no longer needed.

2. Malicious Client Applications

A malicious client application is a client application that has been intentionally designed to steal a user's data or credentials. Malicious client applications can be created by attackers who seek to obtain unauthorized access to a user's protected resources. These applications may look and function like legitimate applications, but they are designed to collect sensitive information such as access tokens, passwords, or other confidential data.

To prevent the use of malicious client applications, OAuth providers should implement a robust client authentication mechanism that verifies the identity of the client application before granting access to the user's resources. OAuth providers can use a variety of authentication mechanisms such as client secrets, public key infrastructure (PKI), or digital signatures to ensure that the client application is legitimate.

Additionally, OAuth providers should carefully review and approve all third-party client applications before granting them access to the OAuth service. This review process should include a thorough analysis of the application's functionality and security controls to ensure that it does not pose a threat to the OAuth system or the user's protected resources.

Furthermore, OAuth providers should continuously monitor client applications for any suspicious behavior, such as unusual access patterns, excessive resource usage, or unauthorized data access. Any suspicious activity should be promptly investigated, and if necessary, the offending client application should be revoked and banned from accessing the OAuth system.

3. Man-in-the-Middle Attacks

Man-in-the-middle (MITM) attacks can intercept the communication between the client application and the authorization server, allowing the attacker to gain access to the user's resources.

A MITM attack is a type of cyberattack where an attacker intercepts the communication between two parties and can modify, redirect or steal the information exchanged between them. In the context of OAuth, a MITM attacker can intercept the communication between the client application and the authorization server, thereby gaining access to the user's protected resources.

To execute a MITM attack on an OAuth implementation, an attacker must be able to intercept the communication between the client application and the authorization server. This can be done by exploiting vulnerabilities in the communication protocol or by gaining access to the network traffic.

To prevent MITM attacks in OAuth implementations, it is crucial to ensure that all communications between the client application and the authorization server are secure and tamper-proof. One way to do this is by implementing secure communication protocols such as HTTPS or SSL/TLS, which encrypt the data transmitted between the client and the server, preventing attackers from intercepting or modifying it.

Additionally, OAuth providers should implement mechanisms such as certificate pinning, which verifies that the certificate presented by the server during the communication is the same as the expected certificate, preventing attackers from impersonating the authorization server.

It is not enough to rely on OAuth providers to protect against man-in-the-middle (MITM) attacks. Users also play a crucial role in preventing these attacks. Therefore, it is essential to educate users about the potential risks of MITM attacks and how to detect and prevent them.

One of the most effective ways to prevent MITM attacks is to use secure networks. Users should be advised to only use trusted networks and avoid using public Wi-Fi or unsecured networks, as these can be easily compromised by attackers. In addition, users should use a VPN (Virtual Private Network) to encrypt their internet traffic and protect their communication from prying eyes.

Furthermore, users should always verify the identity of the OAuth provider and client application before granting access to their protected resources. Users should only authorize applications that they trust and have a legitimate reason for accessing their data. They should also carefully review the permissions requested by the application and only grant the minimum permissions necessary for the application to function.

It is also important to stay vigilant and monitor for any suspicious activity. Users should regularly review their account activity and report any unauthorized access or suspicious behavior to the OAuth provider immediately.

4. Cross-Site Request Forgery (CSRF)

Cross-Site Request Forgery (CSRF) attacks are a type of security vulnerability that can affect OAuth implementations. In a CSRF attack, an attacker tricks a user into performing a specific action without their knowledge or consent. This can include granting access to a malicious client application, changing a user's account settings, or performing a transaction on behalf of the user.

To execute a CSRF attack, the attacker typically sends a request to the OAuth service that appears to be legitimate but is actually malicious. The request includes the user's access token, which the attacker obtained by tricking the user into visiting a malicious website or clicking on a malicious link. Once the request is processed, the attacker gains access to the user's protected resources.

To prevent CSRF attacks, OAuth providers should implement measures that verify the authenticity of the request. One of the most effective ways to do this is to include a CSRF token in the OAuth request. This token is a randomly generated value that is unique to each request and is verified by the OAuth service before processing the request. If the token is missing or invalid, the request is rejected, and the user is not granted access to the protected resources.

In addition to implementing CSRF tokens, OAuth providers should also educate users about the risks of CSRF attacks and how to detect and prevent them. Users should be advised to only click on links from trusted sources and to avoid clicking on links or buttons that they do not recognize. They should also ensure that their browser is up-to-date and that they are using a security plugin that blocks malicious websites and scripts.

Finally, OAuth providers should continuously monitor their systems for any suspicious activity, including unusual access patterns, excessive resource usage, or unauthorized data access. Any suspicious activity should be promptly investigated, and if necessary, the offending user or application should be revoked and banned from accessing the OAuth system.

4.2 Best Practices for Securing OAuth

1. Use HTTPS

OAuth communication should be encrypted using HTTPS to prevent eavesdropping and MITM attacks.

HTTPS, or Hypertext Transfer Protocol Secure, is an extension of HTTP that adds encryption and authentication mechanisms using SSL/TLS. It uses digital certificates to establish a secure connection between the client application and the servers, preventing eavesdropping, tampering, and impersonation attacks.

By using HTTPS, all OAuth communication between the client application, authorization server, and resource server is encrypted and protected from unauthorized access. This includes the exchange of authorization codes, access tokens, refresh tokens, and other sensitive information.

Using HTTPS also helps prevent man-in-the-middle (MITM) attacks, where an attacker intercepts and modifies the communication between the client and the servers. Without HTTPS, an attacker can easily intercept the communication and steal user credentials or access tokens, or inject malicious code into the OAuth flow.

2. Use Secure Storage

One of the critical aspects of securing OAuth is ensuring that access tokens and refresh tokens are stored securely. These tokens provide access to user data and resources, and if they fall into the wrong hands, they can be used to impersonate users or gain unauthorized access to their accounts.

To prevent token leakage, it is essential to store access tokens and refresh tokens securely. This means storing them in a way that makes it difficult or impossible for attackers to access them.

One best practice for secure storage of tokens is to use cryptographic mechanisms such as encryption and hashing. Access tokens and refresh tokens can be encrypted using strong encryption algorithms and stored in a secure database or file system. Similarly, the use of one-way hash functions can be used to store tokens in a way that is irreversible, making it difficult for attackers to obtain the original token value.

Another best practice for secure storage is to restrict access to the token storage system. This can be achieved by implementing access controls such as role-based access control (RBAC) or attribute-based access control (ABAC). These mechanisms ensure that only authorized personnel or processes can access the token storage system, preventing unauthorized access or modification of tokens.

In addition to using encryption, hashing, and access controls, it is also essential to regularly monitor the token storage system for any suspicious activity. This can include monitoring access logs, auditing user activity, and implementing intrusion detection and prevention systems.

By following these best practices for secure storage, you can prevent token leakage and ensure that access tokens and refresh tokens remain confidential and protected from unauthorized access.

3. Verify Client Identity

Verifying the identity of the client application is a critical step in securing OAuth. Without proper client authentication or a whitelist of trusted client applications, an attacker can impersonate a client application and obtain access to user resources.

There are two main ways to verify the identity of the client application: client authentication and whitelist of trusted clients.

Client authentication involves the client application providing credentials, such as a client ID and client secret, to the authorization server when requesting an access token. The authorization server can then verify these credentials to ensure that the client application is authorized to access the requested resources. This process helps prevent unauthorized access by ensuring that only trusted client applications can access user resources.

A whitelist of trusted clients involves maintaining a list of client applications that are authorized to access user resources. When a client application requests access to a user's resources, the authorization server checks the whitelist to ensure that the client application is authorized to access the requested resources. This process can be less secure than client authentication, as it relies on the maintenance of a current and accurate whitelist of trusted client applications.

By implementing client authentication or a whitelist of trusted clients, the authorization server can verify the identity of the client application before granting access to a user's resources. This helps prevent unauthorized access and protects user data.

4. Use Appropriate Grant Types

Using appropriate grant types is another important best practice for securing OAuth. The OAuth 2.0 framework defines several grant types, each with its own strengths and weaknesses. It is important to choose the appropriate grant type based on the requirements of the client application.

For example, the Implicit grant type is designed for client-side applications, such as those running in a web browser. This grant type allows the client application to obtain an access token directly from the authorization server without involving a backend server. However, this grant type does not provide a client secret, which can make it less secure for server-side applications that need to keep sensitive information secret.

On the other hand, the Authorization Code grant type is designed for server-side applications that have a secure backend. This grant type involves a multi-step process that includes obtaining an authorization code, exchanging the authorization code for an access token, and optionally refreshing the access token. This grant type provides a client secret and can be more secure for server-side applications.

By using the appropriate grant type for the application's requirements, the client application can obtain access to user resources in a secure and reliable way. It is important to carefully consider the strengths and weaknesses of each grant type and choose the one that best meets the application's needs.

4.3 Handling Errors and Exceptions

In any software implementation, it is inevitable that errors and exceptions will occur. This is also true for OAuth implementations. However, it is important to handle these errors and exceptions carefully in order to maintain the security of the system. In this chapter, we will discuss some best practices for handling errors and exceptions in OAuth.

Firstly, it is important to ensure that error messages do not contain any sensitive information that could be used to exploit the system. This means that error messages should be generic and not reveal any implementation details. For example, an error message could simply state that an invalid client ID was provided, without providing any further details that could be used to exploit the system.

Secondly, OAuth providers should ensure that the error response is consistent across all endpoints. This means that the error response should have the same structure and format regardless of the endpoint that generated the error. This helps to ensure that errors are handled consistently and that attackers cannot exploit differences in the error response to gain access to sensitive information.

Thirdly, OAuth providers should ensure that errors are logged and monitored. This helps to identify any patterns or trends in the types of errors that are occurring, which can be used to improve the overall security and stability of the system.

Finally, OAuth providers should ensure that exceptions are handled gracefully. This means that exceptions should be caught and handled in a way that does not compromise the security of the system. For example, if an exception occurs during the authentication process, the user should be redirected to an error page rather than being provided with sensitive information that could be used to exploit the system.

In conclusion, error handling is a crucial part of securing OAuth implementations. OAuth providers should ensure that error messages are generic, error responses are consistent, errors are logged and monitored, and exceptions are handled gracefully. By following these best practices, OAuth providers can improve the security and stability of their systems.

Chapter 5: Advanced Topics

OAuth is a widely used protocol for secure authentication and authorization of client applications to access user's protected resources on various platforms. It is an open standard that provides a framework for secure and delegated access to protected resources by client applications. In this chapter, we will discuss some advanced topics of OAuth, including custom grant types, device flow, JSON Web Tokens (JWT), token introspection, and token revocation.

5.1 Custom Grant Types

Custom grant types are a powerful extension to the OAuth protocol that can be used to create customized authentication and authorization flows for specific use cases. The standard OAuth grant types are designed to cover the most common use cases, such as web applications or mobile apps, but sometimes more specialized requirements are needed.

OAuth extension grant specification allows developers to define their own grant types by specifying new endpoints, parameters, and response formats. This enables developers to create custom flows that meet the specific needs of their applications.

For instance, a company that is building a medical application might need to authenticate users by checking their medical credentials before granting access to sensitive data. In such a scenario, the company can define a custom grant type that performs the necessary authentication checks before issuing an access token.

Custom grant types can be beneficial for complex use cases that require specialized authentication and authorization flows, but developers should be cautious when using them. Custom grant types can introduce new security vulnerabilities that must be carefully evaluated and mitigated. It is important to ensure that the custom grant type is properly secured and does not introduce any security weaknesses into the overall OAuth system.

Developers should also be mindful of the compatibility issues that can arise when using custom grant types. Custom grant types are not standardized, and therefore may not be recognized by all OAuth providers or clients. Developers should test their custom grant types thoroughly to ensure they work correctly across different environments and scenarios.

5.2 Device Flow

The device flow is a specialized OAuth flow that enables users to authorize access to their protected resources using a separate device when the device itself is not capable of using traditional authentication methods. This is particularly useful for devices such as smart TVs, gaming consoles, and IoT devices that do not have a web browser or other conventional means of user interaction.

In the device flow, the device requesting access to the user's resources displays a URL and a code to the user. The user then goes to a separate device, such as a smartphone or computer, and navigates to the URL provided. This device then prompts the user to enter the code displayed on the original device.

The browser on the second device then contacts the authorization server to initiate the authentication process. Once the user is authenticated, the authorization server generates an access token that is sent back to the browser on the second device.

Finally, the user enters the access token into the original device, which uses it to access the protected resources. This process is typically designed to be easy for the user to complete, even if they are not familiar with the OAuth protocol or are using a device with limited capabilities.

The device flow provides an additional layer of security compared to traditional OAuth flows because the user must physically interact with two devices in order to complete the authentication process. This helps prevent unauthorized access to the user's resources and ensures that only authorized users can access protected resources.

5.3 JSON Web Tokens (JWT)

JSON Web Tokens (JWTs) are a type of token that is widely used for securely transmitting information between parties. They have become a popular way to represent claims because they are compact, self-contained, and can be used to transmit information securely between parties, such as client applications and OAuth providers.

JWTs consist of three parts: a header, a payload, and a signature. The header contains information about the type of token and the algorithm used to sign it. The payload contains the claims or information that the token represents. The signature is used to verify the authenticity of the token.

In OAuth, JWTs can be used to represent access tokens and refresh tokens. This has several advantages over traditional token formats. First, because JWTs are self-contained, they eliminate the need for an OAuth provider to store access and refresh token information in a database. This reduces the amount of storage and processing required by the OAuth provider and can improve performance. Second, JWTs can be signed with a secret key, which makes it possible to verify the authenticity of the token without requiring access to the OAuth provider's database. This improves the security of the system by reducing the risk of token forgery or tampering.

To use JWTs in OAuth, the OAuth provider must support them as a token format. Clients can then request JWT access tokens and use them to access protected resources. The OAuth provider can verify the authenticity of the token by checking the signature, and can use the claims in the token to determine the access level of the client.

In addition to their use in OAuth, JWTs are also commonly used for transmitting authentication and authorization information in other contexts. They have become a popular format for representing claims because of their compactness, portability, and security features.

5.4 Token Introspection

Token introspection is a crucial part of securing OAuth implementations. It allows resource servers to validate access tokens and ensure that only authorized parties can access protected resources. When a resource server receives an access token from a client application, it can use token introspection to verify that the token is valid and has not been revoked or expired.

Token introspection involves sending a request to the OAuth provider's introspection endpoint. This request includes the access token and any necessary authentication credentials. The OAuth provider then checks the access token's status and returns information about its validity, such as the token's expiration time and scope of access.

Token introspection can be used for various purposes, such as auditing and monitoring access to protected resources. It can also help detect and prevent unauthorized access attempts, such as when a client application tries to use a revoked access token to access protected resources.

5.5 Token revocation

Token revocation is another important security feature of OAuth. It allows users to revoke access to a client application or invalidate a compromised access token. This can be achieved by implementing token revocation using various methods, including OAuth 2.0 Token Revocation RFC or maintaining a blacklist of revoked tokens.

OAuth 2.0 Token Revocation RFC provides a standard mechanism for revoking access tokens. It defines a revocation endpoint that can be used to revoke access tokens, refresh tokens, or both. To revoke a token, a client application sends a revocation request to the OAuth provider's revocation endpoint, including the access token or refresh token and any necessary authentication credentials. The OAuth provider then revokes the token and updates its status accordingly.

5.6 Maintaining a backlist

Maintaining a blacklist of revoked tokens is another approach to token revocation. When a user revokes access to a client application, or when an access token has been compromised or stolen, the OAuth provider can add the token to a blacklist. The blacklist is essentially a database or list of revoked tokens that are no longer valid.

When a client application sends a request to the OAuth provider using an access token, the provider can check the blacklist to determine if the token has been revoked. If the token is found on the blacklist, the provider can deny the request, preventing the client application from accessing the user's resources.

The blacklist approach has some advantages over other methods of token revocation. It allows for more granular control over which tokens are revoked, as individual tokens can be added or removed from the blacklist. This can be useful in cases where only a single token needs to be revoked, rather than revoking all tokens for a particular client application.

However, the blacklist approach also has some drawbacks. Maintaining a large blacklist can be resource-intensive, as the provider must continually update the list with revoked tokens. Additionally, the blacklist approach may not be suitable for distributed systems, as the blacklist must be accessible to all resource servers that need to verify access tokens.

OAuth provides a flexible and secure framework for client applications to access protected resources on various platforms. Advanced topics such as custom grant types, device flow, JSON Web Tokens (JWT), token introspection, and token revocation can enhance the security and functionality of OAuth implementations. By understanding and implementing these advanced topics, developers can create more secure and robust OAuth systems.

Chapter 6: Integration with popular platforms

OAuth is widely used by popular platforms such as Facebook, Twitter, Google, and GitHub to provide secure access to their resources through third-party applications. Integration with these platforms using OAuth can simplify the authentication and authorization process for developers and users alike. In this chapter, we will explore how OAuth is integrated with these popular platforms.

6.1 Facebook

Facebook uses OAuth 2.0 for authentication and authorization. Developers can use the Facebook Graph API to access Facebook resources, such as user profiles and photos. To use the Facebook API, developers must first register their application with Facebook and obtain an App ID and App Secret. Then, the application must redirect the user to the Facebook authentication page, where they will be prompted to grant access to the application. Once the user grants access, Facebook returns an access token that the application can use to access the user's resources.

6.2 Twitter

Twitter uses OAuth 1.0a for authentication and authorization. To use the Twitter API, developers must first register their application with Twitter and obtain a Consumer Key and Consumer Secret. Then, the application must redirect the user to the Twitter authentication page, where they will be prompted to grant access to the application. Once the user grants access, Twitter returns an access token and secret that the application can use to access the user's resources.

6.3 Google

Google uses OAuth 2.0 for authentication and authorization. Google offers various APIs, such as Google Drive, Google Calendar, and Google Maps, that developers can use to access Google resources. To use the Google APIs, developers must first register their application with Google and obtain a Client ID and Client Secret. Then, the application must redirect the user to the Google authentication page, where they will be prompted to grant access to the application. Once the user grants access, Google returns an access token that the application can use to access the user's resources.

6.4 GitHub

GitHub uses OAuth 2.0 for authentication and authorization. Developers can use the GitHub API to access GitHub resources, such as repositories and user profiles. To use the GitHub API, developers must first register their application with GitHub and obtain a Client ID and Client Secret. Then, the application must redirect the user to the GitHub authentication page, where they will be prompted to grant access to the application. Once the user grants access, GitHub returns an access token that the application can use to access the user's resources.

6.5 Other popular platforms

OAuth is also widely used by other popular platforms, such as LinkedIn, Instagram, and Dropbox. These platforms use OAuth in a similar way to the platforms mentioned above, with the developer registering their application, redirecting the user to the authentication page, and obtaining an access token to access the user's resources.

OAuth has become an industry-standard protocol for authentication and authorization, and integration with popular platforms has made it easier for developers to access resources and build applications. The integration process typically involves registering the application, redirecting the user to the authentication page, and obtaining an access token. By understanding how OAuth is integrated with popular platforms, developers can leverage these integrations to build secure and robust applications that can access user resources.

Chapter 7: Future of OAuth

OAuth has become the de facto standard for authentication and authorization on the web, but it is not without its limitations. As technology continues to evolve, there are emerging trends and technologies that could shape the future of OAuth.

7.1 Emerging Trends and Technologies

Decentralized identity systems are a new approach to digital identity that aims to give users more control over their personal data and privacy. These systems use blockchain technology and other decentralized technologies to create a trustless, secure, and user-centric identity system. In such systems, users own and control their identity, rather than relying on a centralized authority or identity provider.

OAuth can play a crucial role in decentralized identity systems by providing a mechanism for authorization and access control. With OAuth, decentralized identity systems can grant access to resources based on user consent and permission. OAuth can also be used to manage access to sensitive user data, such as personal information, medical records, and financial data.

Another emerging trend in OAuth is the use of machine learning and artificial intelligence (AI) to improve the security and performance of OAuth implementations. Machine learning and AI can be used to detect and prevent fraudulent activity, such as bots and fake accounts, and to optimize the OAuth authorization process. For example, machine learning algorithms can be used to analyze user behavior and detect abnormal activity patterns that may indicate a security breach or unauthorized access.

7.2 Potential Improvements to OAuth

Despite its widespread adoption and success, OAuth is not perfect, and there are still opportunities for improvement. Some potential areas for improvement in OAuth include:

1. **Better user experience**

   OAuth can be challenging for users to understand and use, especially for non-technical users. Improving the user experience of OAuth can help to increase adoption and reduce the risk of user errors and security vulnerabilities.

2. **Improved security**

   While OAuth is a secure protocol, there are still some security vulnerabilities and risks associated with it. Improvements to OAuth's security features can help to reduce the risk of attacks and improve the overall security of OAuth implementations.

3. **Better integration with other protocols**

   OAuth is often used in conjunction with other authentication and authorization protocols, such as OpenID Connect and SAML. Improving the integration of OAuth with these protocols can help to create a more seamless and integrated authentication and authorization ecosystem.

7.3 Other Authentication and Authorization Protocols

While OAuth is currently the most widely used authentication and authorization protocol, there are other protocols that are gaining popularity and may offer some advantages over OAuth in certain contexts. These protocols include:

1. **OpenID Connect**

   OpenID Connect is an authentication protocol that is built on top of OAuth. It provides additional authentication features, such as identity verification and user authentication, which can be useful in some contexts.

2. **Security Assertion Markup Language (SAML)**

   SAML is an XML-based protocol that is used for exchanging authentication and authorization data between parties. It is commonly used in enterprise environments and can provide a more centralized and integrated approach to authentication and authorization.

3. **FIDO2**

   FIDO2 is an open standard for passwordless authentication that uses public-key cryptography and biometric authentication methods. It offers a more secure and user-friendly alternative to traditional passwords and can be used in conjunction with OAuth for enhanced security and usability.

OAuth has come a long way since its introduction in 2006 and has become the de facto standard for authentication and authorization on the web. However, there is still room for improvement, and emerging trends and technologies, such as decentralized identity systems and machine learning, offer exciting opportunities for the future of OAuth. Additionally, other authentication and authorization protocols, such as OpenID Connect and SAML, may offer some advantages over OAuth in certain contexts and should be considered alongside OAuth when designing authentication and authorization systems.

7.4 Microservices architectures

Another emerging trend is the use of OAuth in the context of microservices architectures. Microservices architectures are a popular approach to building complex and scalable applications. They are based on the idea of breaking down a large application into smaller, loosely coupled services that can be developed, deployed, and maintained independently. Each service has its own unique functionality and communicates with other services through APIs.

One of the key challenges of microservices architectures is securing the communication between services. OAuth can play a role in securing microservices architectures by providing a mechanism for authorization and access control. Each service can act as an OAuth client, requesting access tokens from an OAuth provider to access protected resources. This ensures that only authorized services can access protected resources and helps to prevent unauthorized access and data breaches.

In the context of microservices architectures, OAuth can also be used to implement fine-grained access control. For example, access tokens can be scoped to specific resources or actions, allowing services to access only the resources they need and reducing the risk of data breaches.

Another benefit of using OAuth in microservices architectures is that it simplifies the management of access control. Rather than implementing access control in each service, access control can be centralized in the OAuth provider. This reduces the complexity of the system and makes it easier to manage access control policies.

As microservices architectures continue to gain popularity, it is likely that OAuth will become an increasingly important technology for securing these architectures. By providing a flexible and scalable mechanism for authorization and access control, OAuth can help to ensure the security and integrity of microservices architectures.

7.5 Potential Improvements to OAuth

There are several potential improvements to OAuth that could enhance its functionality and security. One of these is the use of multi-factor authentication (MFA). Multi-factor authentication (MFA) is a method of authentication that requires the user to provide at least two separate forms of identification before being granted access to a resource. The use of MFA in OAuth could greatly enhance the security of OAuth-based systems by requiring users to provide additional authentication factors beyond their username and password.

One potential approach to incorporating MFA into OAuth is through the use of an additional grant type that supports MFA. This grant type would require the user to provide an additional authentication factor in order to obtain an access token. For example, the user might be prompted to enter a one-time code sent to their mobile device in addition to their username and password.

Another potential improvement to OAuth is the use of more advanced encryption algorithms to secure the transmission of access tokens. While OAuth already supports secure transmission of tokens using SSL/TLS, there is always room for improvement. The use of more advanced encryption algorithms, such as post-quantum cryptography, could provide an even higher level of security against attacks.

Additionally, some have suggested that OAuth could benefit from better support for resource access control. While OAuth provides a mechanism for granting access to protected resources, it does not provide a way to enforce fine-grained access controls. Enhancements to OAuth that better support resource access control could help to address this limitation and provide a more secure and flexible authorization framework.

7.6 Token binding

Token binding is a proposed improvement to the OAuth protocol that aims to increase the security of access tokens. It involves binding an access token to a specific client device or browser using a cryptographic key. This makes it more difficult for attackers to steal and reuse access tokens, as the token is only valid for a specific device.

Token binding works by generating a key pair on the client device, consisting of a private key and a public key. The public key is then sent to the authorization server during the OAuth flow, along with the access token request. The authorization server uses the public key to generate a token binding ID, which is then included in the access token. The client device stores the private key, which is used to prove the authenticity of the token binding ID during subsequent requests.

The use of token binding can help prevent token theft and replay attacks, as the access token is only valid for a specific device. If an attacker steals an access token, they will not be able to use it on another device, as the token binding ID will not match. This makes it more difficult for attackers to gain unauthorized access to protected resources.

While token binding is not yet widely implemented in OAuth, it is a promising improvement that can enhance the security of the protocol. The OAuth working group is currently working on a token binding specification for OAuth 2.1, which is expected to include support for token binding.

7.7 Other Authentication and Authorization Protocols

While OAuth is widely used, there are other authentication and authorization protocols that could challenge its dominance in the future. One of these is OpenID Connect. OpenID Connect (OIDC) is an authentication protocol that is built on top of OAuth 2.0. It provides a way for users to authenticate themselves to web applications and share their identity information securely. One of the key benefits of OpenID Connect is that it provides a standardized way for developers to implement authentication and authorization in their applications.

OpenID Connect provides several features that make it an attractive alternative to OAuth, particularly for enterprise applications. One of these features is single sign-on (SSO), which allows users to log in to multiple applications using a single set of credentials. This can simplify the authentication process for users and improve the user experience.

Another key feature of OpenID Connect is session management. This feature allows web applications to manage user sessions across multiple devices and across different applications. This can improve security by ensuring that users are logged out of all applications when they log out of one application.

OpenID Connect also provides additional identity information about the user, such as their name and email address. This can be useful for applications that require more detailed user information. In addition, OpenID Connect supports user consent, which allows users to control which applications have access to their identity information.

Another authentication and authorization protocol that could challenge OAuth in the future is the Security Assertion Markup Language (SAML). SAML is an XML-based protocol that is used to exchange authentication and authorization data between different systems. SAML is widely used in enterprise environments and is supported by many identity providers, such as Microsoft Active Directory and Okta.

One of the key benefits of SAML is its support for federation, which allows organizations to share identity information securely with partners and other organizations. SAML also supports SSO, which can improve the user experience and simplify the authentication process for users.

While OAuth is currently the dominant authentication and authorization protocol, it is possible that OpenID Connect and SAML could gain popularity in the future, particularly in enterprise environments. Developers and organizations should stay informed about emerging authentication and authorization protocols and consider their specific needs when selecting a protocol for their applications.

7.8 FIDO

Another protocol that could challenge OAuth is FIDO (Fast Identity Online).

FIDO (Fast Identity Online) is an emerging authentication protocol that is gaining popularity as an alternative to traditional password-based authentication systems. FIDO is based on public-key cryptography and is designed to provide secure, private, and easy-to-use authentication for online services.

One of the main benefits of FIDO is that it eliminates the need for passwords, which are a common target for cyber attacks such as phishing, credential stuffing, and brute force attacks. Instead of passwords, FIDO uses a combination of biometric factors (such as fingerprints or facial recognition) and/or hardware tokens (such as USB keys or smart cards) to authenticate users.

FIDO consists of two main protocols: FIDO UAF (Universal Authentication Framework) and FIDO2. FIDO UAF allows users to authenticate using biometric factors, while FIDO2 allows users to authenticate using hardware tokens.

FIDO is gaining support from major tech companies such as Google, Microsoft, and Apple, and is being adopted by a growing number of online services. FIDO is also being integrated with existing authentication and authorization protocols such as OAuth and OpenID Connect, allowing for seamless and secure authentication across multiple services and platforms.

While FIDO offers many benefits over traditional password-based authentication systems, it is still in its early stages of adoption and implementation. As with any emerging technology, there are challenges to be addressed, such as ensuring interoperability between different FIDO implementations, and ensuring that FIDO is accessible to users with disabilities or who do not have access to biometric devices.

OAuth has become a critical component of modern web and mobile applications, providing a secure and reliable way to handle authentication and authorization. As technology continues to evolve, there are emerging trends and technologies that could shape the future of OAuth. Additionally, there are potential improvements to OAuth that could enhance its functionality and security. However, there are also other authentication and authorization protocols that could challenge the dominance of OAuth in the future. It is important for developers to stay up-to-date with these trends and technologies to ensure that they are building secure and reliable applications.

Chapter 8: Implementing OAuth Step-by-Step

A Step-by-Step Guide to Implementing OAuth in Your Application

OAuth is a powerful tool for enabling secure authorization and access control in your application. In this chapter, we will walk you through the process of implementing OAuth in your application, step by step.

Step 1: Register Your Application

The first step in implementing OAuth in your application is to register your application with the OAuth provider. This typically involves creating an account with the provider and providing some basic information about your application, such as its name and a redirect URL.

Each OAuth provider has its own registration process, but the basic steps are usually similar. Once your application is registered, you will receive a client ID and client secret, which you will use to authenticate your application when making OAuth requests.

Step 2: Obtain Authorization

The next step is to obtain authorization from the user. This involves redirecting the user to the OAuth provider's authorization endpoint, where they will be asked to grant your application access to their protected resources.

To initiate the authorization process, you will need to redirect the user to a URL that includes the OAuth provider's authorization endpoint, your client ID, and the redirect URL you specified when registering your application. The user will be prompted to log in to the OAuth provider and grant your application access to their resources.

Once the user has granted authorization, the OAuth provider will redirect them back to your application's redirect URL, along with an authorization code.

Step 3: Exchange Authorization Code for Access Token

With the authorization code in hand, your application can now exchange it for an access token. To do this, your application sends a request to the OAuth provider's token endpoint, including the authorization code, client ID, client secret, and redirect URL.

The OAuth provider will validate the authorization code and, if it is valid, will respond with an access token. The access token is a long, random string that your application will use to access the user's protected resources.

Step 4: Access Protected Resources

With an access token in hand, your application can now access the user's protected resources. To do this, your application includes the access token in requests to the OAuth provider's resource endpoint.

The OAuth provider will validate the access token and, if it is valid, will respond with the requested resource. Your application can then use the resource as needed.

Step 5: Handle Access Token Expiration and Revocation

Access tokens typically expire after a set period of time, and users may revoke access to your application at any time. To handle these scenarios, your application will need to periodically check the expiration status of the access token and handle any errors that occur when attempting to access protected resources with an expired or revoked token.

In this chapter, we have walked you through the process of implementing OAuth in your application, step by step. By following these steps, you can enable secure authorization and access control in your application, while also providing a seamless user experience.

Chapter 9: Avoid Common Pitfalls

While OAuth is a powerful and widely used protocol, there are several common pitfalls that can result in security vulnerabilities or other issues. In this chapter, we will discuss some of these pitfalls and how to avoid them.

1. **Insecure Token Storage**

   One of the most common pitfalls of OAuth is storing access tokens in an insecure manner. If an attacker gains access to an access token, they can use it to access protected resources. To avoid this, access tokens should be stored in a secure manner, such as using encryption or hashing.

2. **Lack of Token Validation**

   Another common pitfall is failing to validate access tokens before granting access to protected resources. Access tokens should be validated to ensure that they have not been tampered with or revoked before granting access to protected resources.

3. **Insufficient Authorization Scope**

   Another pitfall is granting excessive authorization scope to an access token. Access tokens should only be granted the minimum authorization scope required to perform their intended functions.

4. Insufficient Client Authentication

Client authentication is an important aspect of OAuth security. If client authentication is not performed correctly, an attacker may be able to impersonate a legitimate client and gain access to protected resources. Therefore, it is important to use strong client authentication mechanisms, such as client secrets or public key cryptography.

5. Inadequate User Consent

In OAuth, user consent is an important aspect of the authorization process. If user consent is not obtained or is obtained in an unclear or misleading manner, users may unwittingly grant access to sensitive information. It is important to obtain clear and explicit user consent before granting access to protected resources.

6. Failure to Monitor and Revoke Access

Finally, it is important to monitor access to protected resources and revoke access when necessary. If access is not monitored, attackers may be able to access protected resources without detection. Similarly, if access is not revoked when necessary, attackers may be able to continue accessing protected resources even after the initial access token has expired.

To avoid these common pitfalls, it is important to follow best practices for implementing OAuth, such as using secure token storage mechanisms, validating access tokens before granting access to protected resources, and obtaining clear and explicit user consent. Additionally, it is important to monitor access to protected resources and revoke access when necessary to prevent unauthorized access.

Chapter 10: Conclusion on OAuth

OAuth is a widely adopted authentication and authorization protocol that allows users to grant third-party applications access to their resources without sharing their credentials. It provides a secure and standardized way for users to authorize access to their resources while maintaining control over their data.

In this chapter, we will recap the key points covered in this guide and provide final thoughts on OAuth.

10.1 Recap of Key Points

Throughout this guide, we have covered various aspects of OAuth, including:

- OAuth is an open standard for authorization that allows users to grant third-party applications access to their resources without sharing their credentials.

- OAuth has three main roles: the resource owner, the client, and the authorization server.

- OAuth 2.0 is the most widely used version of OAuth and includes several grant types, such as the authorization code grant, implicit grant, and client credentials grant.

- OAuth can be integrated with popular platforms such as Facebook, Twitter, Google, and GitHub.

- There are potential improvements to OAuth, such as the use of multi-factor authentication (MFA) and token binding.

- Other authentication and authorization protocols such as OpenID Connect and FIDO could challenge OAuth's dominance in the future.

10.2 Final Thoughts on OAuth

OAuth is a powerful and flexible protocol that enables secure and user-friendly authorization for third-party applications. It has become an essential component of many modern applications and systems, providing a standard way for users to authorize access to their resources without sharing their credentials.

While OAuth has its limitations and potential security vulnerabilities, it remains a robust and reliable framework for authentication and authorization. By following best practices and keeping up to date with emerging trends and technologies, developers can ensure that their OAuth implementations remain secure and effective.

In conclusion, OAuth is a critical technology that enables secure and user-friendly authorization for modern applications and systems. Its widespread adoption and versatility ensure that it will continue to play an essential role in the authentication and authorization landscape for years to come.

X References for further reading about OAuth:

1. OAuth 2.0 specifications: https://tools.ietf.org/html/rfc6749

2. OAuth.net, the official website for OAuth: https://oauth.net/

3. "OAuth 2.0 in Action" by Justin Richer and Antonio Sanso (Manning Publications, 2017)

4. "OAuth 2.0 Identity and Access Management Patterns" by Matthias Biehl (Apress, 2019)

5. "OAuth 2.0 Cookbook" by Adolfo Eloy Nascimento (Packt Publishing, 2018)